Completely

DIANE  WARREN

Usually the person who writes a foreword like this does so because
of great admiration. In this particular case, I'm writing
this foreword because of pure unadulterated jealousy.

Every time I hear a Diane Warren song, I turn green.
How can anybody seem to be able to turn out a hit song at will?
Diane has the uncanny ability to take everyday, relatable
situations and turn them into songs with universal appeal. Her
songs are so potent because just about everyone can identify with
what she says in them.

I'm sure you, as I, have sat down on occasion and have tried to put
thoughts into words and music, I have been around music all my
life. I've always harbored the thought, "if 'so and so' can do it, then
I ought to be able to do it". I've tried. Believe me, it's not easy.
The talent that Diane has belongs to a select few. Obviously, it's
God-given. The overwhelming majority of us haven't been so blessed.

I have extraordinary admiration for this wonderful and talented
woman. I do envy her, but not seriously. I thank her for making
such a magnificent contribution to us through her music.
Diane Warren is truly special.

Dick

Dick Clark

David Geffen

Diane Warren is a muse who has the ability to see into the heart of all of us and each of us at the same time. Her soulful lyrics and enchanting melodies capture our most personal emotions. It's no wonder that her songs are sung and heard and loved the world over.

Patty Austin

Every time I sing "Any Other Fool" in concert and the audience is singing along I am amazed at your ability to tap into the human spirit. Thank you for the opportunity to share your genius with the world. Love Patti

Kenny G

I still don't know how she does it. She talks like a veteran truck driver and then turns around and writes these beautiful songs. Someone please explain this to me!!!

Ed Eckstine

In 1981, I was the General Manager of Quincy Jones organization. One of my functions was to interface with the song writing and publishing communities and I used to spend time at the Los Angeles Songwriters Showcase which was the great well-spring of young, unencumbered song writing talent in L.A.. A girlfriend of mine at the time was a member of Lass and her best friend in the budding songwriter world was Diane Warren.

David Foster

When I think of Diane Warren many words come to mind but the one that sticks out more than any other is "Hit". "Hit" because she has written so many and "Hit" because I'd like to hit her for writing so many!!!

Of course, I'm joking about the latter but of the first, I truly believe she is the premier pop songwriter of our time. But don't take just my word for it. Ask the huge array of superstars that have benefitted from her work. She is enormously talented, incredibly determined and she writes the songs the whole world sings. I feel very privileged to be amongst the many record producers that she looks to in helping her get her songs on tape.

We love you and your work Diane!!! Don't stop writing or a lot of us will be out of a job! (Of course then maybe I would be forced to record my own songs)- hey, not a bad idea...Naaahhh.

Dion

Each night I ask the stars up above

Celine Dion

Every time I record a Diane Warren song, I am lifted to a higher level, and that feeling returns every time I perform her songs live.

Bette Midler

I've probably spoken more to Diane Warren's mom than to Diane. Her mom is crazy about me, and I'm crazy about Diane. What a song!

She used to say that one day Diane would be the biggest songwriter in the business and I was a knuckle head for not paying more attention to her and seeing that the future pop Laureate was right in front of my eyes. Her prophecy became reality and now Diane doesn't return my phone calls when I'm groveling for hits! I value our friendship tremendously.

Shanice Wilson

Diane Warren is truly one of the best songwriters in the business. She is so down to earth and a lot of fun to be around. Diane is so real and personable, which makes working with her so easy. Though I admire many qualities about her, the one that I admire most is her creativity. You are the best.

Gloria & Emilio Estefan

Seldom have we met a songwriter who can work with such depth and expression as Diane Warren. Her ability to illustrate life through her music is a gift we have all been fortunate to share.

Maxi Priest

The first time I met Diane, I thought she was very funny, and very humorous. She has a real down to earth sense of humor, I immediately felt comfortable which is most important for me. I had a great time bringing her lyrics to life, working with Roberta Flack and Arif Mardin...It was exciting. Like the first day at a new school. I'd just like to wish her continued success. Hopefully we'll work together again someday, that would be an honor and a pleasure.

Michael Bolton

Diane is like a little sister to me - a sister I'd like to lock up in the closet - but then she'd probably start humming some irresistible melody and I'd have to let her out to write the song.

Irving Azoff

Not many people can make it on talent alone, though Diane Warren certainly could. What makes her so amazing is how hard she works after her music has been recorded. Whatever the case, her songs are always wonderful and they're always hits. With love and thanks...Irving Azoff

Aaron Neville

"Don't Take Away My Heaven" is one of the best songs of the past couple of years. Lately almost all of the love songs out there are "lust" songs. "Don't Take Away My Heaven" is a pure love song. Diane is a great songwriter, and I can't wait to do more of her songs in the future.

Expose

The three of us consider ourselves very fortunate to have worked with such a talented, outgoing, loony, bad joke telling, crazy person such as you. We are looking forward to the next time we work together. Thanks for the great songs!...Love, Ann, Kelly and Jeanette.

Michael W. Smith

Diane Warren is without a doubt one of the most gifted songwriters of our time. Her music has provided a backdrop for our culture. Diane, thanks for being there for so many.

Why can't I write songs like Diane Warren

Clive Davis

I know we share the same passion for music, and its been a wonderfully fulfilling experience to participate with you in bringing your music to millions all over the world. Thanks for your zest, your hunger, your creativity and your friendship...Love Clive

Grace Slick

"Realsongs" - The name of her company - right! My first impression of Diane - This woman is REAL. No attitude (except when need for hard ball black humor). No arrogance (God knows she deserves to flash a dose) - no Rodeo Drive duds (she can afford to buy the whole street). Easy to know, easy to like, and she can put into music what we all try to feel - love is the final answer...yup.

Charles Koppelman

As a professional, Diane amazes with her tenacity and disarms with her wit. As a writer, she is at once prolific beyond imagination, lyrically unequaled and a master of melody. As a publisher, she has an unerringly keen sense of casting for her songs. Simply put, she sets a standard to emulate. Congratulations, Diane, on this impressive body of work.

Eric Carmen

Writing a great song is hard. Writing two or three is harder. But writing a lot of great songs that consistently become hits and standards over a couple of decades is next to impossible. Relatively few songwriters have ever been able to do it. But those that have, have become legends and Diane is destined to take her place alongside them.

As a friend and collaborator I can tell you she's the perfect combination of raw talent, inspiration and hard work. Keep'em comin', Di. The world can never have too many great songs.

El DeBarge

From the first day I met Diane up to the last time I saw her, she was a nut and still is! I appreciate her sense of humor although I know it's probably too rough for some because mine is, and we both have the same sense of humor. To be such a wonderful songwriter is a true gift from God and to have benefited from such a gift as Dianes is true love. Love you Lady Di, El

Kathy Troccoli

I used to read writing credits on records- Diane Warren, Diane Warren, Diane Warren...so many songs I loved with your name attached to them. I would dream of singing one some day. Then it happened and "Everything Changed". Thank you, Diane. You have my deep admiration. You're the best.

Roberta Flack

When I heard Diane's demo tape of "Set The Night To Music", I was speechless. I knew it was special, and I could hear Maxi and I singing it. I am honored and privileged to sing anything she writes. There's a unique quality about her songs: They're definitely hers, but can never be anticipated. She is absolutely, in my opinion, the ultimate songwriter...Roberta Flack, April 1994

Contents

Completely

Words and Music by
DIANE WARREN

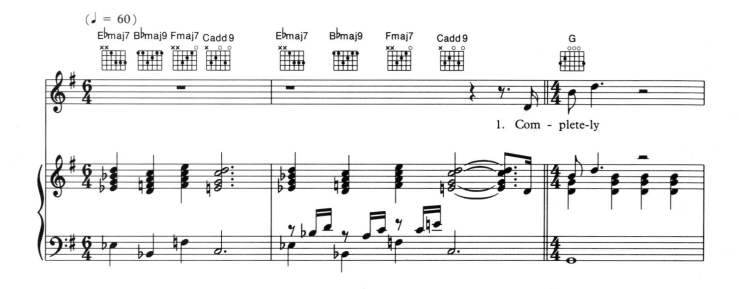

1. Com - plete-ly

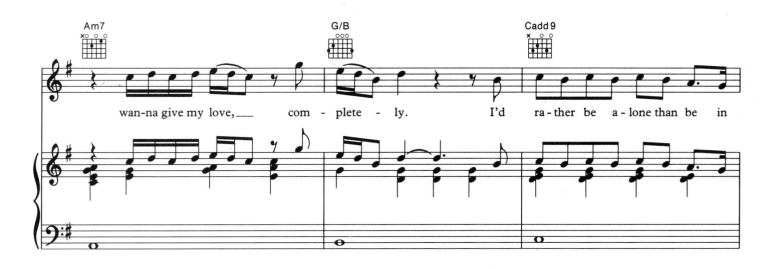

wan-na give my love,___ com - plete - ly. I'd ra - ther be a - lone than be in

love just half the way. I want to find some-one that I can trust com -

Love Will Lead You Back

Words and Music by
DIANE WARREN

I'll Never Get Over You Getting Over Me

Words and Music by
DIANE WARREN

Moderate ballad

I hear you're tak-ing the town — a-gain, — hav-ing a good time with all your

By The Time This Night Is Over

Words and Music by
DIANE WARREN, ANDY GOLDMARK
and MICHAEL BOLTON

Every Road Leads Back To You

Words and Music by
DIANE WARREN

Old friend,___ here we are, af-ter all the years and tears___ and all___ that we've___ been through.___
Old friend,___ there were times I did-n't want to see your face___ or hear___ your name a-gain.___

It feels___ so good___ to see___ you.
Now those times are far___ be-hind___ me. It's

If I Could Turn Back Time

Words and Music by
DIANE WARREN

Water From The Moon

Words and Music by
DIANE WARREN

Time, Love And Tenderness

Words and Music by
DIANE WARREN

Rhythm Of The Night

Words and Music by
DIANE WARREN

Don't Turn Around

Words and Music by
DIANE WARREN and ALBERT HAMMOND

Swear To Your Heart

**Words and Music by
DIANE WARREN**

As Long As I Can Dream

Words and Music by
DIANE WARREN and ROY ORBISON

Everything Changes

Words and Music by
DIANE WARREN

Well you came _____ in my life _____ like a ray
er would be _____ an - y - one

I Will Be Here For You

Words and Music by
DIANE WARREN and MICHAEL W. SMITH

Missing You Now

Words and Music by
DIANE WARREN,
MICHAEL BOLTON and WALTER AFANASIEFF

If You Asked Me To

Words and Music by
DIANE WARREN

Moderately slow

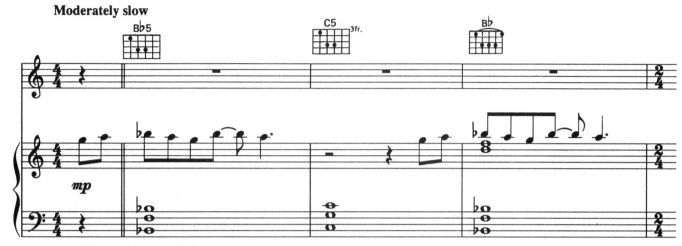

With pedal as needed

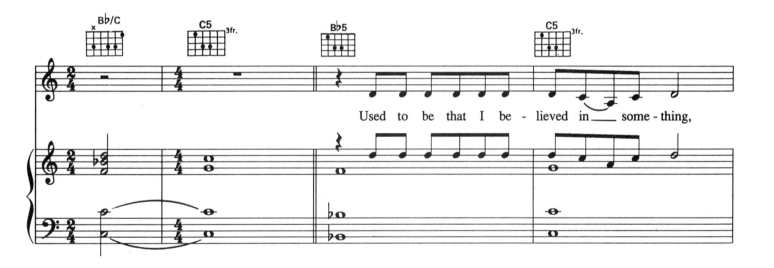

Used to be that I be - lieved in ____ some - thing,

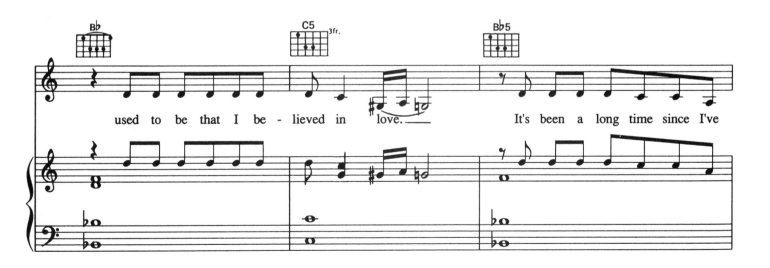

used to be that I be - lieved in love. ____ It's been a long time since I've

Christmas Through Your Eyes

Words and Music by
DIANE WARREN and GLORIA ESTEFAN

Verse 2:
I see the rain, you see the rainbow hiding in the clouds.
Never afraid to let your love show, won't you show me how?
Wanna learn how to believe again,
Find the innocence in me again, through your young heart.
Help me find a way, help me try.
(To Chorus:)

Don't Take Away My Heaven

Words and Music by
DIANE WARREN

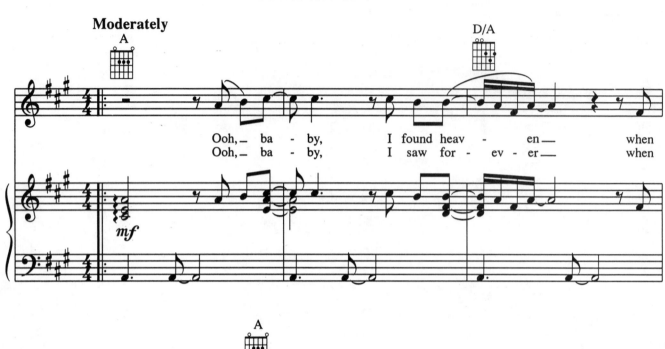

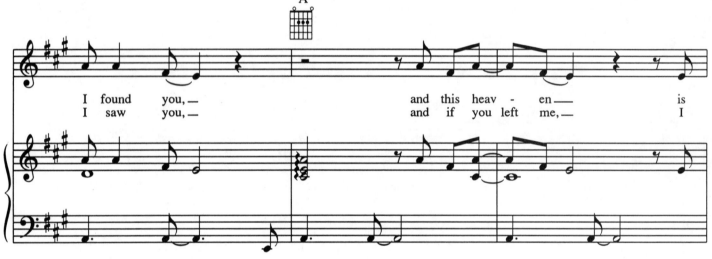

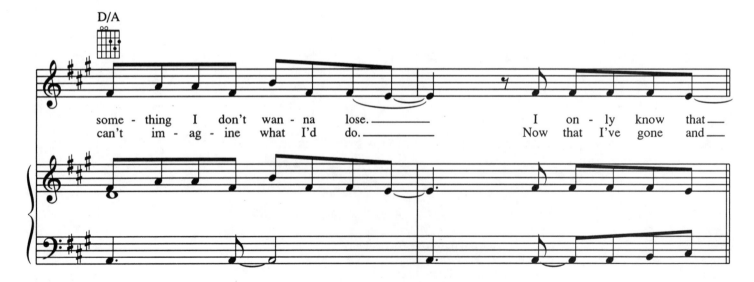

Any Other Fool

Words and Music by
DIANE WARREN and ROBBIE BUCHANAN

had it all— when you— were lov-ing me,— (Had all— the love— I'd ev-er

had it all— as an-y fool— could see,— an-y oth-er fool but me.—
need.)

Look Away

**Words and Music by
DIANE WARREN**

Moderately slow

Well, you called me up— this morn-ing, told me 'bout the
both a-greed— as lov-ers, we were

new love you found, I said I'm hap-py for— you.
bet-ter off as friends, that's how it had to be,— yeah.

I'm real-ly
That's how it

Nothing Broken But My Heart

Words and Music by
DIANE WARREN

I've been o—ver you
You won't see—no tears—

for some time
in my eyes—

— now, ba—by.
— now, ba—by.

I don't miss—your kiss like be—fore
If you think—I'm sad that you're gone—

ba - by,___ since you left___ me you might think that___ my world's been

torn a - part.___ But if you see me,___ ba - by, you'll see that

noth - ing's bro - ken, noth - ing bro - ken but my heart.

heart.___ You might think___

Love And Understanding

Words and Music by
DIANE WARREN

Set The Night To Music

Words and Music by
DIANE WARREN

ic._____

The mo - ment is ours_ to take,_____

When The Night Comes

Words and Music by
DIANE WARREN,
JIM VALLANCE and BRYAN ADAMS

I know there'll be a time for you and I, just take my hand and run a-

way, pick up all the piec- es of this

shat- tered dream, we're gon- na make it ours some- day, that's when we're

D.S. % *al Coda* ⊕

com- in' back, com- in' back to stay.

Love Can Move Mountains

Words and Music by
DIANE WARREN

Live For Loving You

Words and Music by
DIANE WARREN,
GLORIA ESTEFAN and EMILIO ESTEFAN, JR.

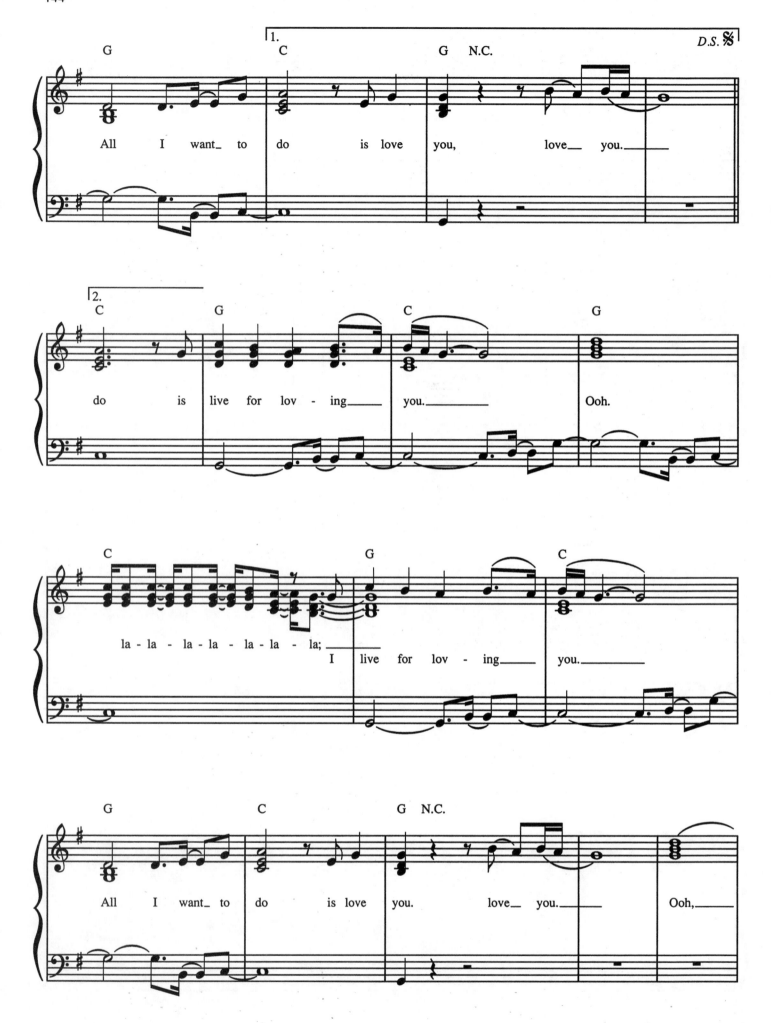

la - la - la - la - la - la - la - la;_____   la - la - la - la - la - la - la;_____

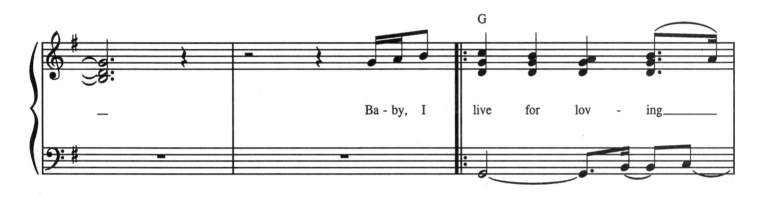

_____   Ba - by, I   live   for   lov - ing_____

Repeat ad lib. and fade

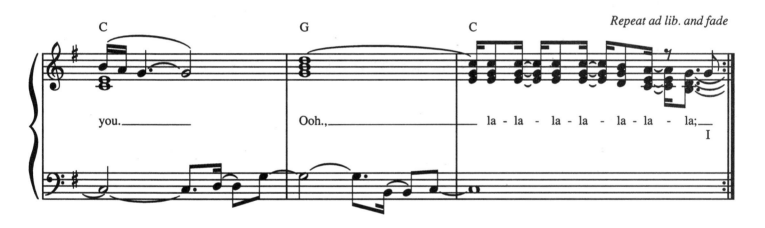

you._____   Ooh.,_____ la - la - la - la - la - la - la;_____
I

Verse 2:
I find it hard to find the words
To say what I am feeling.
I'm so in love, I'm so alive,
And I know you're the reason why,
Why I'm so happy all the time.
Oh, I, I wonder, wonder, wonder why.
(To Bridge:)

Verse 3:
It would never cross my mind,
To find another lover.
'Cause after having been with you,
There could be no other.
I, just touching you I'm satisfied.
Oh, I, I wonder, wonder, wonder why.
(To Bridge:)

Saving Forever For You

From BEVERLY HILLS, 90210 Soundtrack

Words and Music by
DIANE WARREN

I've nev-er been__ so sure__ a-bout__ an-y-thing be-fore,__ but this
You'll be my world__ as long__ as there's a world turn-in' 'round.__ And you'll

love I'm feel-ing gon-na be a feel-ing I'll feel for-ev-er more.__
be my heav-en, ba-by, 'til the heav-ens all come fall-ing down.__

Nothing's Gonna Stop Us Now

Words and Music by
DIANE WARREN
and ALBERT HAMMOND

Look - ing in your eyes I see__ a par - a - dise, this world__
__ so glad I found you, I'm__ not gon - na lose you, what ev -

__ that I found__ is too good__ to be true.__ Stand - ing here be - side you, want__
er it takes__ I will stay__ here with you.__ Take__ you to the good times, see__

When I See You Smile

Words and Music by
DIANE WARREN

Moderately fast

legato

mf

Some- times I won- der if I'd ev - er make it through,_ through this world_ with- out hav- ing you._

When I see you smile, ____

1. ba - by, when I see you ____ smile at ____ me.

2. ba - by, when I see you smile ____ at me. Some - times ____ I wan - na

When I see you smile

I can face the world. _ Oh, _____ you know

I can do an-y-thing. __ When I